I0430202

CONTENTS

MAP OF TOGO

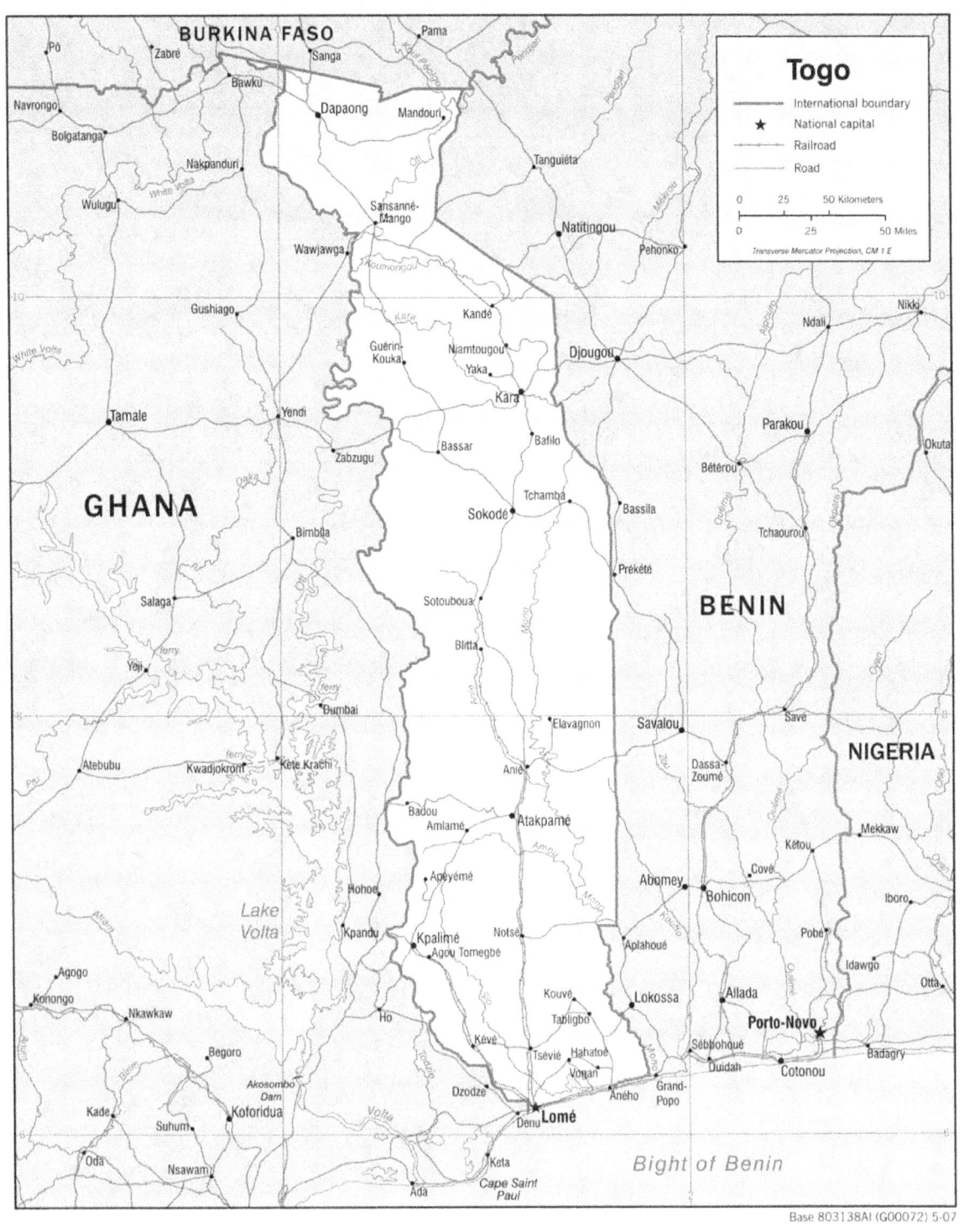

Base 803138AI (G00072) 5-07

PEACE CORPS/TOGO
HISTORY AND PROGRAMS

History of the Peace Corps in Togo

The Peace Corps began its work in Togo in 1962, as part of the second wave of countries where the Peace Corps began service. Since that time, more than 2,500 Volunteers have served in Togo. Peace Corps/Togo has a successful history of collaboration and involvement with the Togolese people at all levels. The Volunteers' efforts build upon counterpart relationships and emphasize low-cost solutions that make maximum use of local resources, which are usually people. Collaboration with local and international private organizations, as well as international development organizations, is an important component of Volunteer project activities.

History and Future of Peace Corps Programming in Togo

Peace Corps/Togo averages 55 trainees per year and fields an average of 110 Volunteers. Volunteers work in all five regions of the country in four programs: natural resource management; community health and AIDS prevention; small enterprise development; and girls' education and empowerment.

Heavy demographic pressure is straining Togo's agricultural systems and the ability of the land to regenerate itself. Traditional farming practices cannot meet the needs of the increasing population, nor do these practices address the problem of soil degradation. Togo's forests are being depleted, while demand for wood products is increasing. Crop residues, a precious organic fertilizer for tropical soils, are no longer left on the land, but are used as alternative fuels. Volunteers in the natural resource management program work to address these issues and attempt to reverse the trends in the areas of decreasing farm yields, environmental degradation, poor soil fertility, and decreasing forest resources.

In 1995, the safe motherhood and child survival project evolved into the community health and AIDS prevention project. Volunteers in this project assist local-level health personnel and regional offices to promote community health activities. The project's most important components are child growth monitoring and nutrition education, family planning education, education for sexually transmitted diseases (STDs)/AIDS prevention, and improved dispensary management.

Since 1991, small enterprise development Volunteers have worked with credit unions, women's informal savings groups, and youth and local nongovernmental organizations (NGOs) to offer business training and consulting to members who wish to improve their business skills. Workshops covering such topics as accounting, finance, marketing, and feasibility studies are offered to groups of tailors, retailers, merchants, market women, and other entrepreneurs. The goal of this project is to improve basic business and entrepreneurial skills, thereby fostering opportunities for growth and job creation in Togo's small business sector. Information and communication technology (ICT) was added to this program in 2006. Volunteers advise and help entrepreneurs, trade associations, and NGOs (including credit unions) take advantage of ICT to improve management and extend outreach.

In 1999, Peace Corps/Togo began implementation of the girls' education and empowerment program in order to respond to the needs expressed by former Volunteers, their counterparts, and Togo government authorities. Volunteers work with local schools, institutions, and workplaces, particularly in rural and urban areas, to promote education among girls. Emphasis is given to encouraging girls to attend and stay in school and to make good choices about their future.

In addition to the four major program areas mentioned above, Volunteers are involved in a variety of secondary activities. Two activities that many Volunteers participate in are youth summer camps and AIDS Ride. AIDS Ride is a weeklong HIV/AIDS awareness raising program. During AIDS Ride Week, teams of Volunteers in each of the five regions of Togo ride their bikes to isolated villages and deliver HIV/AIDS training sessions to adults and students. In 2008, 80 Volunteers (five teams of 16) delivered 114 presentations in 94 villages to over 32,400 people.

During school vacation each summer, partners and Volunteers from all programs participate in four weeks of youth camps (one week each for girls, boys, and student apprentices). These camps include formal classes in life skills, such as health and nutrition, HIV/AIDS and gender equity, as well as sports and other games. These camps, named Camp UNITE (Initiative for Unification of the Nation through Work and Education), bring students and apprentices from throughout the country to a central location for one week for every category of participants.

Togo's gender and development (GAD) committee was created in 1992 to address gender issues in the work of Volunteers and to incorporate gender awareness into all Peace Corps/Togo programs.

COUNTRY OVERVIEW: TOGO AT A GLANCE

History

When Germany lost control of its former colonies after World War I, part of Togoland was ceded to the British in the then-Gold Coast (now Ghana). The remainder of the territory came under French control and became an independent Togo in 1960. In 1963 the country's first elected president was killed in a coup d'état, Africa's first. In 1967, Gnassingbe Eyadema became president and remained in the position until February 2005, when he suddenly died of a heart attack. Eyadema was Africa's longest-serving head of state. His son, Faure Gnassingbe, became president of Togo in April 2005.

Togo continues to experience profound political challenges. After nearly three decades of one-party rule by President Eyadema and the Rassemblement du Peuple Togolais (Assembly of Togolese People, or RPT), the Constitution was changed to permit the registration of other political parties. Though the RPT continues to overwhelmingly dominate the government, there is a great deal of pressure for change from within the country and from outside agencies such as the World Bank and the European Union. As a result of the legislative elections of October 2007, political tension eased even more as opposition parties now hold seats in parliament. With these new political developments, the EU and international organizations continue to resume aid programs.

Government

The Togolese government is headed by the president and consists of numerous ministries and an elected legislative body. The country is divided into five regions, and each region is divided into prefectures, the loose equivalent of counties. All political officials are appointed by the government.

Economy

Togo's coastal location, the best port in the sub-region, and better-than-average infrastructure, have helped to make Lomé (the capital) a regional trading center. However, agriculture is the foundation of Togo's economy, contributing 30 percent of the country's gross domestic product (GDP) and employing 70 percent of its workers. Corn, sorghum, millet, cassava, yams, cowpeas, and rice are the major food crops. Cash crops include cotton, cocoa, and coffee. Togo is the world's fifth-largest producer of phosphates. Industry and manufacturing account for about a quarter of Togo's GDP. Half of the total domestic output is accounted for in the service sectors.

Note that the Economist Intelligence Unit provides generally accurate and comprehensive (and updated) political and economic news of Togo.

People and Culture

For such a small country, there is an amazing number of ethnic groups and over 60 local languages are spoken. The official language is French, and the two principal local languages are Ewé (the predominant language of the south that is also spoken in Ghana and Benin) and Kabyé (the predominant language of the north). Togolese communities are close and based on a network of extended family and other members of the community. Sharing is very much the norm.

Animism or fetishism is practiced by a large number of Togolese – even those converted to other religions such as Islam and Christianity.

Environment

Togo's position on the African continent and its proximity to the equator place it in a rain shadow. During the rainy season severe floods can occur, as they did in the north in 2007 and in the south in 2008. Togo was once covered with dry land forests, but most of these are gone—the result of agricultural expansion and the need for wood over the centuries. Traveling from south to north, the change in climate and environment for each region is readily apparent, from the humid coast to the semiarid north.

There never were the vast concentrations of wildlife that most Americans associate with Africa—or more specifically, East Africa. Most of the indigenous species are gone, due to human population pressures on the land and hunting practices. Togo does have some areas set aside for national parks, but increasing pressure for farmland is reducing the size of these areas.

RESOURCES FOR FURTHER INFORMATION

Following is a list of websites for additional information about the Peace Corps and Togo and to connect you to returned Volunteers and other invitees. Please keep in mind that although we try to make sure all these links are active and current, we cannot guarantee it. If you do not have access to the Internet, visit your local library. Libraries offer free Internet usage and often let you print information to take home.

A note of caution: As you surf the Internet, be aware that you may find bulletin boards and chat rooms in which people are free to express opinions about the Peace Corps based on their own experience, including comments by those who were unhappy with their choice to serve in the Peace Corps. These opinions are not those of the Peace Corps or the U.S. government, and we hope you will keep in mind that no two people experience their service in the same way.

General Information About Togo

🕮 **www.countrywatch.com/**

On this site, you can learn anything from what time it is in the capital of Togo to how to convert from the dollar to the Togolese CFA. Just click on Togo and go from there.

🕮 **www.lonelyplanet.com/destinations**

Visit this site for general travel advice about almost any country in the world.

🕮 **www.state.gov**

The State Department's website issues background notes periodically about countries around the world. Find Togo and learn more about its social and political history. You can also go to the site's international travel section to check on conditions that may affect your safety.

- ❧ **www.psr.keele.ac.uk/official.htm**

  This includes links to all the official sites for governments worldwide.

- ❧ **www.geography.about.com/library/maps/blindex.htm**

  This online world atlas includes maps and geographical information, and each country page contains links to other sites, such as the Library of Congress, that contain comprehensive historical, social, and political background.

- ❧ **www.cyberschoolbus.un.org/infonation/info.asp**

  This United Nations site allows you to search for statistical information for member states of the U.N.

- ❧ **www.worldinformation.com**

  This site provides an additional source of current and historical information about countries around the world.

Connect With Returned Volunteers and Other Invitees

- ❧ **www.rpcv.org**

  This is the site of the National Peace Corps Association, made up of returned Volunteers. On this site you can find links to all the Web pages of the "Friends of" groups for most countries of service, comprised of former Volunteers who served in those countries. There are also regional groups that frequently get together for social events and local volunteer activities. Or go straight to the Friends of Togo site: www.friendsoftogo.org/.

- ❧ **www.PeaceCorpsWorldwide.org**

  This site is hosted by a group of returned Volunteer writers. It is a monthly online publication of essays and Volunteer accounts of their Peace Corps service.

Recommended Books

- ❧ Decalo, Samuel. *Historical Dictionary of Togo*. 3rd Edition. Metuchen, N.J., Scarecrow Press. 1996.

- ❧ *Foreign Economic Trends and Their Implications: Togo*. Latest Edition. Washington, D.C., Dept. of Commerce, International Trade Administration.

- ❧ Kourouma, Ahmadou. *Waiting for the Vote of the Wild Animals*. University Press of Virginia. 2001 (Translated from French).

Lewis, Tom and Jungman, Robert. *On Being Foreign: Culture Shock in Short Fiction.* Intercultural Press. 1986.

Newton, Alex. *West Africa, A Travel Survival Kit.* Alex Newton. Berkeley, Calif., Lonely Planet. 1988.

Packer, George. *The Village of Waiting.* New York, N.Y.: Farrar, Straus and Giroux; 1 edition. 2001.

Piot, Charles. Remotely Global: *Village Modernity in West Africa.* Chicago, University of Chicago Press.

Books About the History of the Peace Corps

Hoffman, Elizabeth Cobbs. *All You Need is Love: The Peace Corps and the Spirit of the 1960s.* Cambridge, Mass.: Harvard University Press, 2000.

Rice, Gerald T. *The Bold Experiment: JFK's Peace Corps.* Notre Dame, Ind.: University of Notre Dame Press, 1985.

Stossel, Scott. *Sarge: The Life and Times of Sargent Shriver.* Washington, D.C.: Smithsonian Institution Press, 2004.

Meisler, Stanley. When the World Calls: The Inside Story of the Peace Corps and its First 50 Years. Boston, Mass.: Beacon Press, 2011.

Books on the Volunteer Experience

Dirlam, Sharon. Beyond Siberia: Two Years in a Forgotten Place. Santa Barbara, Calif.: McSeas Books, 2004.

Casebolt, Marjorie DeMoss. Margarita: A Guatemalan Peace Corps Experience. Gig Harbor, Wash.: Red Apple Publishing, 2000.

Erdman, Sarah. Nine Hills to Nambonkaha: Two Years in the Heart of an African Village. New York, N.Y.: Picador, 2003.

Hessler, Peter. River Town: Two Years on the Yangtze. New York, N.Y.: Perennial, 2001.

Kennedy, Geraldine ed. From the Center of the Earth: Stories out of the Peace Corps. Santa Monica, Calif.: Clover Park Press, 1991.

Thompsen, Moritz. Living Poor: A Peace Corps Chronicle. Seattle, Wash.: University of Washington Press, 1997 (reprint).

LIVING CONDITIONS AND VOLUNTEER LIFESTYLE

Communications

Mail

The postal system in Togo is good by regional standards. However, it is nowhere near as efficient as the U.S. postal system. In general, letters will take two to five weeks to arrive, sometimes longer depending on a myriad of influences as diverse as seasonal slowdowns to Paris airport strikes. Packages will take longer; large packages sent surface mail have been known to take six months to a year to arrive. You should tell family and friends to send only small packages under 5 pounds and always to use airmail. There are import duties levied on packages arriving in Togo based on the stated value of the contents. A well-insured package, while more likely to arrive intact, will cost you much more on this end and is not the best option. It is not unheard of to receive packages already opened and with items missing or damaged.

There is a regular weekly Express Mail Service (EMS) for Volunteers between the Peace Corps office in Lomé and several mail points throughout Togo. Besides EMS, Volunteers in some cities have their own post office boxes, individually, or as a group.

During your pre-service training and throughout your service you may receive letters and packages at the following address:

PCT / PCV "your name"
Corps de la Paix
B.P. 3194
Lomé, Togo
West Africa

Telephones

Togo has a fairly good communications system. A telephone system links all the regional and district capitals, and these lines are fairly reliable (except during the rainy season, when breakdowns do happen). The telephone systems in Lomé and within other urban areas are reliable, and there is work in progress to double the capacity of these systems.

Peace Corps Volunteers can easily communicate via telephone with their families. This does not mean you will have a telephone available at your site, but all regional capitals offer good phone service to the U.S. Phone service continues to improve as more and more *cabines* (telephone booths) set up shop throughout the country. Volunteers generally arrange in advance to receive phone calls from people in the United States, which makes it much less expensive than calling the United States from Togo. Volunteers are not permitted to make personal calls from the Peace Corps office in Lomé, but they may receive calls there. Collect calls, or calls to 1-800 numbers, cannot be made from Togo to the United States.

There is a five-hour time difference between Togo and the U.S. East Coast (four during Daylight Savings Time).

Cell phone reception is expanding throughout Togo and most Volunteers end up buying cell phones locally. However, owning a cell phone is not required by Peace Corps and can sometimes be expensive on a Volunteer allowance. Furthermore, there is no guarantee of cell phone reception at individual Volunteer sites.

There are fax lines linking Togo with other countries all over the world. Lomé has most of the fax capability, but some regional capitals have fax lines as well.

Computer, Internet, and Email Access

Internet service providers operate in Togo and Internet cafés are becoming more readily available all over the country. Internet phone availability provides a cheaper option than landlines. Internet connections are very slow and prices vary. Do not expect to be able to download anything.

Housing and Site Location

Volunteers in Togo are provided housing as part of the community's contribution to their work. Most Togo Volunteers live in villages in a two- or three-room house, most likely in a compound with a Togolese family. Some Volunteer houses have tin roofs; a few have straw roofs. It is unlikely that you will have running water or electricity, although they are more common in larger city posts. Water sources in villages can be traditional wells, bore-holes equipped with pumps, cisterns, and natural water sources—in some cases, rivers. Whatever your source of drinking water, you will have to treat it before use.

Living Allowance and Money Management

As a Volunteer, you receive a monthly living allowance of 129,000 CFA, roughly equivalent to $285—sufficient to live at a modest level in your community. You will also receive a settling-in allowance to defray the initial costs of setting up a household. Both allowances are paid in local currency. The living allowance is deposited into Volunteers' bank accounts on a quarterly basis, which means you have to manage your money well to avoid running out before the end of the quarter. Many Volunteers' bank accounts are in one of the five regional capitals, which means you will normally take at least one trip to the regional capital each month. It is inadvisable to keep large sums of money at home.

In case of emergency, there are also Visa and MasterCard ATMs in Lomé, while Western Union can be found nearly everywhere.

Food and Diet

Your diet will consist of locally grown foods or a combination of local and imported tinned foods. A typical Togolese meal is a carbohydrate-base rice, yams, pâte (boiled corn meal or flour) or fufu (pounded white yams), accompanied by a variety of hot, spicy sauces. Rice and beans, usually eaten at breakfast, is another common meal. Meat is available throughout Togo, but it is expensive; fresh fish is only available in larger towns.

Fruits and vegetables are seasonal, occasionally making it difficult for vegetarians to adhere to a sound diet, especially in the more remote areas. Some Volunteers plant vegetable gardens to supplement their diet. If not, you can find most of your food in the nearest cities or weekly markets. Smaller villages often provide only basic food supplies. You may need to travel to larger towns for vegetables and specific items, especially during dry season.

Take advantage of your host family's hospitality during pre-service training (PST, also referred to as "stage" in French). Learn how to cook, see how ingredients can be reinterpreted, etc.

Transportation

Togo's main national highway runs the length of the country. Most of the road is in good condition, but some parts are in poor repair. There are several other sections of paved road, some in good condition, others not. Most of the local roads in Togo are sand or dirt—very dusty in the dry season, very muddy in the rainy season, and full of potholes.

You will be given an all-terrain bicycle and helmet for your transportation needs at your site. Failure to wear a helmet can result in administrative separation from the Peace Corps.

When traveling around the country, you will use varying types of transportation. Lomé has many private taxis. Taxis also travel frequently between Lomé and the larger towns in the interior. This taxi travel tends to be fairly irregular and uncomfortable, but always interesting.

Use of motorcycles by Peace Corps Volunteers is generally prohibited. However, there is a transportation policy in Togo, allowing a few specific Volunteers in isolated posts to ride as passengers on motorcycles while traveling to their sites. These Volunteers must wear motorcycle helmets, provided by the Peace Corps.

Distance from the villages to the prefectoral and regional capitals may be anywhere from 10 to 60 kilometers. While some Volunteers like biking these distances, others prefer taking local public transportation, such as bush taxis, to the nearest mail point, bank, or shopping location.

The bottom line, and unfortunately the reality of life in Togo, is that travel is inherently more risky here than what one would experience using public transportation in the United States. Peace Corps Volunteers find that their bikes are sufficient for most work-related travel. In addition, Volunteers are clustered so that most are within a bike ride of another Volunteer. It is usually necessary, however, to use local transport (e.g., bush taxis) when traveling long distances. By and large, the vehicles (usually mini-buses or Toyota station wagons) are old and poorly maintained, and it is unlikely that many of the drivers will win safe-driving awards anytime soon!

Peace Corps/Togo provides a shuttle bus service (Lomé Limo) that runs from the north of the country to the capital and back once a month. The Peace Corps encourages Volunteers to limit transport via bush taxi. When it is necessary to use bush taxis, you are encouraged to select what appears to be the safest vehicle available and to go with drivers whose driving habits are known and reasonable. When you find yourself in what you consider an unsafe situation (e.g., a driver traveling too fast despite having been asked to slow down), you should demand to be let out of the vehicle immediately. Your experiences in public transport can increase your understanding of local realities (e.g., maybe people are late to your meetings because of the challenges of local transport). The best strategy, however, is to minimize travel via public transport and to avoid all nighttime travel.

Geography and Climate

Togo is a small country on the West African coast. Only 50 kilometers wide in sections, it stretches 600 kilometers inland from the Gulf of Guinea to the savanna of Burkina Faso in the north. Situated between Ghana to the west and Benin to the east, it is roughly the size of West Virginia. Togo supports a diverse population of nearly 5 million and has more than 50 ethnic groups and languages.

Togo's geography is mainly savanna-like, although some areas in the center of the country are fairly hilly. The rainy season lasts from June to September in the north and from May to October in the south. The rest of the year is dry and dominated by dry harmattan winds coming off the Sahara. Temperatures range from the 70s and 80s in the south, to the 80s and 90s in the north. In the months before the rains, the temperatures are higher, reaching the low hundreds in the north.

Social Activities

Togolese are extremely social, and most social activities center around community events. Various ceremonies and "fêtes" are held throughout the year and Volunteer attendance is always well appreciated. In addition, Volunteers get together on different occasions, even if it is just for a regional meeting. Your social life will be as busy as you care to make it.

Professionalism, Dress, and Behavior

Togolese, like people everywhere, will make judgments about you in terms of how you act and how you dress. Dress in the West African context is a sign of respect and professionalism—you show respect for colleagues by how you dress. While appropriate dress and behavior will be discussed during pre-service training, you should also take cues from your colleagues once you are at your site. Togolese business attire—at least outside Lomé—tends to be more casual than in the United States. You will find, however, that your Togolese counterparts are invariably well groomed and wear pressed, clean clothing. Tight, form-fitting clothing for women or clothing exposing the stomach, back, shoulders or knees is almost never appropriate. The same is true for shorts and rubber flip-flops for both men and women during professional meetings, whether in your village or in the regional capital.

To guide you, Peace Corps Togo Volunteers have established the following dress code for work situations:

1. No shorts

2. No "tapette-style" (i.e., rubber) flip-flops

3. No halters/spaghetti straps, etc. for women

4. Collared shirts for men/clean T-shirts

5. Supply of shoes/clothes in Volunteer lounge at the office.

Examples of formal work situations: Everywhere in the office, excluding PCV lounge, "sensibilisations" (i.e. community trainings), Peace Corps trainings with counterparts, Peace Corps Volunteer training and pre-service training.

Please note that in a work situation professional women do not wear clothes that reveal their shoulders or knees.

Personal Safety

More detailed information about the Peace Corps' approach to safety is contained in the "Health Care and Safety" chapter, but it is an important issue and cannot be overemphasized. As stated in the Volunteer Handbook, becoming a Peace Corps Volunteer entails certain safety risks. Living and traveling in an unfamiliar environment (oftentimes alone), having a limited understanding of local language and culture, and being perceived as well-off are some of the factors that can put a Volunteer at risk. Many Volunteers experience varying degrees of unwanted attention and harassment. Petty thefts and burglaries are not uncommon, and incidents of physical and sexual assault do occur, although most Togo Volunteers complete their two years of service without incident. The Peace Corps has established procedures and policies designed to help you reduce your risks and enhance your safety and security. These procedures and policies, in addition to safety training, will be provided once you arrive in Country X. Using these tools, you are expected to take responsibility for your safety and well-being.

Each staff member at the Peace Corps is committed to providing Volunteers with the support they need to successfully meet the challenges they will face to have a safe, healthy, and productive service. We encourage Volunteers and families to look at our safety and security information on the Peace Corps website at **www.peacecorps.gov/safety.**

Information on these pages gives messages on Volunteer health and Volunteer safety. There is a section titled "Safety and Security —Our Partnership." Among topics addressed are the risks of serving as a Volunteer, posts' safety support systems, and emergency planning and communications.

Rewards and Frustrations

What is considered a challenge or a reward varies from person to person, but certainly you will find yourself having to adapt to different perceptions, for example, of time and productivity. Female Volunteers will have to deal with the reality that Togo is very much a patriarchal society, meaning that men are generally accorded more power and respect than women. You may spend a lot of the time being totally baffled as to why things are turning out as they are.

The potential rewards, however, far outweigh any challenges. You will almost inevitably find yourself part of a close-knit community, unlike anything you have experienced in America. You will receive the satisfaction of being able to share your good fortune with those less fortunate and knowing that you are participating in the most pressing development issues that Togo faces: including the fight against HIV/AIDS and poverty. By the end of your two years of service, you will find that you have grown immeasurably and have become a citizen of the world.

The Peace Corps is not for everyone. Your personal flexibility, creativity and optimism, your commitment to work within your community to improve conditions, and your desire to promote human understanding across cultural barriers will be the basis for overcoming many of the physical and emotional challenges which you will face during your assignment in Togo. Acceptance into a foreign culture and the acquisition of a second or even third language are significant rewards. You should carefully consider your decision to come to Togo based on the information contained in this booklet.

Your commitment to the Peace Corps Togo program is of paramount importance.

PEACE CORPS TRAINING

Pre-Service Training

Training is held in communities that are as similar as possible to the typical site for a given project. You will quickly learn to call your PST by its French name "Stage" (pronounced "stahge"). You will live with a host family. Other trainees from your program will live in the same village, but each of you will have your own host family. All of your language, technical, cross-cultural and community development, and personal health and safety sessions will take place either in your host village or a neighboring community. Current Volunteers are available during PST to assist in training and to answer your questions.

Training days are long and demanding, so be prepared. Your day will start at 7:30 a.m. and continue until 5:30 p.m., with a two-hour break for lunch and other short breaks throughout the day. On Saturdays, you will have classes from 7:30 a.m. until noon. Training is an essential part of your Peace Corps service. Our goal is to give you sufficient skills and information to prepare you for living and working in Togo. Pre-service training uses an experiential approach wherever possible. Rather than reading and/or hearing about Volunteer activities, you will be practicing, processing, and evaluating actual or simulated activities.

The 11 weeks of pre-service training are divided into two phases. Phase I runs for the first six weeks and is very intensive in French language and cultural training. Additionally, there are sessions on safety and security, medical/health, and some technical training. This first phase will help you develop basic language and cultural adaptation skills.

Phase II is also very intensive, but it centers on technical training. Language classes will continue, and technical material will increasingly be presented and practiced in French. Some trainees will begin local language classes during this phase, depending on their level of French. Safety and security training and medical/health training also continue.

During the second or third week of training, your associate Peace Corps director (APCD) will interview you about possible sites to help identify a post that is linked to your skills, interests, and needs. During the seventh or eighth week, you will spend a week at your site. This will be your first contact with your future site and will provide an idea of what real Volunteer life is like, what work options exist, and an opportunity to know more of Togo. It also gives you a break from the intense, structured regime of the pre-service training schedule.

Technical Training

Technical training will prepare you to work in Togo by building on the skills you already have and helping you develop new skills in a manner appropriate to the needs of the country. The Peace Corps staff, Togo experts, and current Volunteers will conduct the training program. Training places great emphasis on learning how to transfer the skills you have to the community in which you will serve as a Volunteer.

Technical training will include sessions on the general economic and political environment in Togo and strategies for working within such a framework. You will review your technical sector's goals and will meet with the Togo agencies and organizations that invited the Peace Corps to assist them. You will be supported and evaluated throughout the training to build the confidence and skills you need to undertake your project activities and be a productive member of your community.

Language Training

As a Peace Corps Volunteer, you will find that language skills are key to personal and professional satisfaction during your service. These skills are critical to your job performance, they help you integrate into your community, and they can ease your personal adaptation to the new surroundings. Therefore, language training is at the heart of the training program. You must successfully meet minimum language requirements to complete training and become a Volunteer. Togo language instructors teach formal language classes five days a week in small groups of four to five people.

Your language training will incorporate a community-based approach. In addition to classroom time, you will be given assignments to work on outside of the classroom and with your host family. The goal is to get you to a point of basic social communication skills so you can practice and develop language skills further once you are at your site. Prior to being sworn in as a Volunteer, you will work on strategies to continue language studies during your service.

Cross-Cultural Training

As part of your pre-service training, you will live with a Togo host family. This experience is designed to ease your transition to life at your site. Families go through an orientation conducted by Peace Corps staff to explain the purpose of pre-service training and to assist them in helping you adapt to living in Togo. Many Volunteers form strong and lasting friendships with their host families.

Cross-cultural and community development training will help you improve your communication skills and understand your role as a facilitator of development. You will be exposed to topics such as community mobilization, conflict resolution, gender and development, nonformal and adult education strategies, and political structures.

Health Training

During pre-service training, you will be given basic medical training and information. You will be expected to practice preventive health care and to take responsibility for your own health by adhering to all medical policies. Trainees are required to attend all medical sessions. The topics include preventive health measures and minor and major medical issues that you might encounter while in Togo. Nutrition, mental health, setting up a safe living compound, and how to avoid HIV/AIDS and other sexually transmitted diseases (STDs) are also covered.

Safety Training

During the safety training sessions, you will learn how to adopt a lifestyle that reduces your risks at home, at work, and during your travels. You will also learn appropriate, effective strategies for coping with unwanted attention and about your individual responsibility for promoting safety throughout your service.

Additional Trainings During Volunteer Service

In its commitment to institutionalize quality training, the Peace Corps has implemented a training system that provides Volunteers with continual opportunities to examine their commitment to Peace Corps service while increasing their technical and cross-cultural skills. During service, there are usually three training events. The titles and objectives for those trainings are as follows:

In-service training: Provides an opportunity for Volunteers to upgrade their technical, language, and project development skills while sharing their experiences and reaffirming their commitment after having served for three to six months.

Midterm conference (done in conjunction with technical sector in-service): Assists Volunteers in reviewing their first year, reassessing their personal and project objectives, and planning for their second year of service.

Close-of-service conference: Prepares Volunteers for the future after Peace Corps service and reviews their respective projects and personal experiences.

The number, length, and design of these trainings are adapted to country-specific needs and conditions. The key to the training system is that training events are integrated and interrelated, from the pre-departure orientation through the end of your service, and are planned, implemented, and evaluated cooperatively by the training staff, Peace Corps staff, and Volunteers.

YOUR HEALTH CARE AND SAFETY IN TOGO

The Peace Corps' highest priority is maintaining the good health and safety of every Volunteer. Peace Corps medical programs emphasize the preventive, rather than the curative, approach to disease. The Peace Corps in Togo maintains a clinic with a full-time medical officer, who takes care of Volunteers' primary health care needs. Additional medical services, such as testing and basic treatment, are also available in Togo at local hospitals. If you become seriously ill, you will be transported either to an American-standard medical facility in the region or to the United States.

Health Issues in Togo

Most tropical diseases are endemic in Togo, and as a Volunteer you must be prepared to learn about health hazards and to take necessary measures to protect yourself from them. Proper food and water treatment, compliance with malaria prophylaxis, good personal hygiene practices, and adherence to personal safety measures are essential to a healthy Volunteer experience. Additionally, you must be willing to adopt appropriate behaviors to protect yourself from HIV 1 and 2 and other sexually transmitted diseases, which are prevalent in Togo.

Helping You Stay Healthy

The Peace Corps will provide you with all the necessary inoculations, medications, and information to stay healthy. Upon your arrival in Togo, you will receive a medical handbook. At the end of training, you will receive a medical kit with supplies to take care of mild illnesses and first aid needs. The contents of the kit are listed later in this chapter.

During pre-service training, you will have access to basic medical supplies through the medical officer. However, you will be responsible for your own supply of prescription drugs and any other specific medical supplies you require, as the Peace Corps will not order these items during training. Please bring a three-month supply of any prescription drugs you use, since they may not be available here and it may take several months for shipments to arrive.

You will have physicals at midservice and at the end of your service. If you develop a serious medical problem during your service, the medical officer in Togo will consult with the Office of Medical Services in Washington, D.C. If it is determined that your condition cannot be treated in Togo, you may be sent out of the country for further evaluation and care.

Maintaining Your Health

As a Volunteer, you must accept considerable responsibility for your own health. Proper precautions will significantly reduce your risk of serious illness or injury. The adage "An ounce of prevention ..." becomes extremely important in areas where diagnostic and treatment facilities are not up to the standards of the United States. The most important of your responsibilities in Togois to take the following preventive measures:

Compliance with malaria prophylaxis, use of mosquito nets, and application of insect repellent are essential to Volunteer health. These are all provided by the Peace Corps. Malaria is a very serious, sometimes fatal, disease. Noncompliance with malaria prevention measures can result in medical or administrative separation. You will receive more information on malaria and prevention practices during pre-service training.

Abstinence is the only certain choice for preventing infection with HIV and other sexually transmitted diseases. You are taking risks if you choose to be sexually active. To lessen risk, use a condom every time you have sex. Whether your partner is a host country citizen, a fellow Volunteer, or anyone else, do not assume this person is free of HIV/AIDS or other STDs. You will receive more information from the medical officer about this important issue.

Many illnesses that afflict Volunteers worldwide are entirely preventable if proper food and water precautions are taken. These illnesses include food poisoning, parasitic infections, hepatitis A, dysentery, Guinea worms, tapeworms, and typhoid fever. Your medical officer will discuss specific standards for water and food preparation in Togo during pre-service training.

Abstinence is the only certain choice for preventing infection with HIV and other sexually transmitted diseases. You are taking risks if you choose to be sexually active. To lessen risk, use a condom every time you have sex. Whether your partner is a host country citizen, a fellow Volunteer, or anyone else, do not assume this person is free of HIV/AIDS or other STDs. You will receive more information from the medical officer about this important issue.

Volunteers are expected to adhere to an effective means of birth control to prevent an unplanned pregnancy. Your medical officer can help you decide on the most appropriate method to suit your individual needs. Contraceptive methods are available without charge from the medical officer.

It is critical to your health that you promptly report to the medical office or other designated facility for scheduled immunizations, and that you let the medical officer know immediately of significant illnesses and injuries.

Women's Health Information

Pregnancy is treated in the same manner as other Volunteer health conditions that require medical attention but also have programmatic ramifications. The Peace Corps is responsible for determining the medical risk and the availability of appropriate medical care if the Volunteer remains in-country. Given the circumstances under which Volunteers live and work in Peace Corps countries, it is rare that the Peace Corps' medical and programmatic standards for continued service during pregnancy can be met.

If feminine hygiene products are not available for you to purchase on the local market, the Peace Corps medical officer in Togo will provide them. If you require a specific product, please bring a three-month supply with you.

Your Peace Corps Medical Kit

The Peace Corps medical officer will provide you with a kit that contains basic items necessary to prevent and treat illnesses that may occur during service. Kit items can be periodically restocked at the medical office.

Medical Kit Contents

- Ace bandages
- Adhesive tape
- American Red Cross First Aid & Safety Handbook
- Antacid tablets (Tums)
- Antibiotic ointment (Bacitracin, Neomycin or Polymycin B)
- Antiseptic antimicrobial skin cleaner (Hibiclens)
- Band-Aids
- Butterfly closures
- Calamine lotion
- Cepacol lozenges
- Condoms
- Dental floss
- Diphenhydramine HCL 25 mg (Benadryl)
- Insect repellent stick (Cutter)
- Iodine tablets (for water purification)
- Lip balm (Chapstick)
- Oral rehydration salts
- Oral thermometer (Fahrenheit)
- Pseudoephedrine HCL 30 mg (Sudafed)
- Robitussin-DM lozenges (for cough)
- Scissors
- Sterile gauze pads
- Tetrahydrozaline eyedrops (Visine)
- Tinactin (antifungal cream)
- Tweezers

Before You Leave: A Medical Checklist

If there has been any change in your health—physical, mental, or dental—since you submitted your examination reports to the Peace Corps, you must immediately notify the Office of Medical Services. Failure to disclose new illnesses, injuries, allergies, or pregnancy can endanger your health and may jeopardize your eligibility to serve.

If your dental exam was done more than a year ago, or if your physical exam is more than two years old, contact the Office of Medical Services to find out whether you need to update your records. If your dentist or Peace Corps dental consultant has recommended that you undergo dental treatment or repair, you must complete that work and make sure your dentist sends requested confirmation reports or X-rays to the Office of Medical Services.

If you wish to avoid having duplicate vaccinations, contact your physician's office to obtain a copy of your immunization record and bring it to your pre-departure orientation. If you have any immunizations prior to Peace Corps service, the Peace Corps cannot reimburse you for the cost. The Peace Corps will provide all the immunizations necessary for your overseas assignment, either at your pre-departure orientation or shortly after you arrive in Togo. You do not need to begin taking malaria medication prior to departure.

Bring a three-month supply of any prescription or over-the-counter medication you use on a regular basis, including birth control pills. Although the Peace Corps cannot reimburse you for this three-month supply, it will order refills during your service. While awaiting shipment—which can take several months—you will be dependent on your own medication supply. The Peace Corps will not pay for herbal or nonprescribed medications, such as St. John's wort, glucosamine, selenium, or antioxidant supplements.

You are encouraged to bring copies of medical prescriptions signed by your physician. This is not a requirement, but they might come in handy if you are questioned in transit about carrying a three-month supply of prescription drugs.

If you wear eyeglasses, bring two pairs with you—a pair and a spare. If a pair breaks, the Peace Corps will replace them, using the information your doctor in the United States provided on the eyeglasses form during your examination. The Peace Corps discourages you from using contact lenses during your service to reduce your risk of developing a serious infection or other eye disease. Most Peace Corps countries do not have appropriate water and sanitation to support eye care with the use of contact lenses. The Peace Corps will not supply or replace contact lenses or associated solutions unless an ophthalmologist has recommended their use for a specific medical condition and the Peace Corps' Office of Medical Services has given approval.

If you are eligible for Medicare, are over 50 years of age, or have a health condition that may restrict your future participation in health care plans, you may wish to consult an insurance specialist about unique coverage needs before your departure. The Peace Corps will provide all necessary health care from the time you leave for your pre-departure orientation until you complete your service. When you finish, you will be entitled to the post-service health care benefits described in the Peace Corps Volunteer Handbook. You may wish to consider keeping an existing health plan in effect during your service if you think age or pre-existing conditions might prevent you from re-enrolling in your current plan when you return home.

Safety and Security—Our Partnership

Serving as a Volunteer overseas entails certain safety and security risks. Living and traveling in an unfamiliar environment, a limited understanding of the local language and culture, and the perception of being a wealthy American are some of the factors that can put a Volunteer at risk.

Property theft and burglaries are not uncommon. Incidents of physical and sexual assault do occur, although almost all Volunteers complete their two years of service without serious personal safety problems.

Beyond knowing that Peace Corps approaches safety and security as a partnership with you, it might be helpful to see how this partnership works. Peace Corps has policies, procedures, and training in place to promote your safety. We depend on you to follow those policies and to put into practice what you have learned. An example of how this works in practice – in this case to help manage the risk of burglary – is:

- Peace Corps assesses the security environment where you will live and work
- Peace Corps inspects the house where you will live according to established security criteria
- Peace Corps provides you with resources to take measures such as installing new locks
- Peace Corps ensures you are welcomed by host country authorities in your new community
- Peace Corps responds to security concerns that you raise
- You lock your doors and windows
- You adopt a lifestyle appropriate to the community where you live
- You get to know neighbors
- You decide if purchasing personal articles insurance is appropriate for you
- You don't change residences before being authorized by Peace Corps
- You communicate concerns that you have to Peace Corps staff

Factors that Contribute to Volunteer Risk

There are several factors that can heighten a Volunteer's risk, many of which are within the Volunteer's control. By far the most common crime that Volunteers experience is theft. Thefts often occur when Volunteers are away from their sites, in crowded locations (such as markets or on public transportation), and when leaving items unattended.

Before you depart for Togo there are several measures you can take to reduce your risk:

- Leave valuable objects in the U.S.
- Leave copies of important documents and account numbers with someone you trust in the U.S.
- Purchase a hidden money pouch or "dummy" wallet as a decoy
- Purchase personal articles insurance

After you arrive in Togo, you will receive more detailed information about common crimes, factors that contribute to Volunteer risk, and local strategies to reduce that risk. For example, Volunteers in Togo learn to:

- Choose safe routes and times for travel, and travel with someone trusted by the community whenever possible

- Make sure one's personal appearance is respectful of local customs

- Avoid high-crime areas

- Know the local language to get help in an emergency

- Make friends with local people who are respected in the community

- Limit alcohol consumption

As you can see from this list, you must be willing to work hard and adapt your lifestyle to minimize the potential for being a target for crime. As with anywhere in the world, crime does exist in Togo. You can reduce your risk by avoiding situations that place you at risk and by taking precautions. Crime at the village or town level is less frequent than in the large cities; people know each other and generally are less likely to steal from their neighbors. Tourist attractions in large towns are favorite worksites for pickpockets.

The following are other security concerns in Togo of which you should be aware:

- Location: Most assaults (53 percent) occurred when Volunteers were in public areas (e.g., street, park, beach, public buildings). Specifically, 36 percent of assaults took place when Volunteers were away from their sites. Most property crimes occurred in the Volunteer's residence or another Volunteer's residence, followed closely by public areas. Forty-eight percent of property crimes occurred when Volunteers were away from their sites

- Time: Assaults usually took place during the evening, between 6 p.m. and 11 p.m. – though the single hour with the largest percentage of assaults was 1:00 a.m. (8 percent). Property crimes were more common in the middle of the day, from noon to 9 p.m.

- Day: Assaults and property crimes were more commonly reported on weekends (48 percent and 49 percent, respectively).

- Absence of others: Assaults and property crimes (64 percent and 53 percent, respectively) occurred more frequently when the Volunteer was alone.

- Relationship to assailant: In most assaults and property crimes (64 percent and 85 percent), the Volunteer did not know or could not identify the assailant.

- Consumption of alcohol: 23 percent of all assaults and 4 percent of all property crimes involved alcohol consumption by Volunteers and/or assailants.

While whistles and exclamations may be fairly common on the street, this behavior can be reduced if you dress conservatively, abide by local cultural norms, and respond according to the training you will receive.

Staying Safe: Don't Be a Target for Crime

You must be prepared to take on a large degree of responsibility for your own safety. You can make yourself less of a target, ensure that your home is secure, and develop relationships in your community that will make you an unlikely victim of crime. While the factors that contribute to your risk in Togo may be different, in many ways you can do what you would do if you moved to a new city anywhere: Be cautious, check things out, ask questions, learn about your neighborhood, know where the more risky locations are, use common sense, and be aware. You can reduce your vulnerability to crime by integrating into your community, learning the local language, acting responsibly, and abiding by Peace Corps policies and procedures. Serving safely and effectively in Togo will require that you accept some restrictions on your current lifestyle.

Support from Staff

If a trainee or Volunteer is the victim of a safety incident, Peace Corps staff is prepared to provide support. All Peace Corps posts have procedures in place to respond to incidents of crime committed against Volunteers. The first priority for all posts in the aftermath of an incident is to ensure the Volunteer is safe and receiving medical treatment as needed. After assuring the safety of the Volunteer, Peace Corps staff response may include reassessing the Volunteer's worksite and housing arrangements and making any adjustments, as needed. In some cases, the nature of the incident may necessitate a site or housing transfer. Peace Corps staff will also assist Volunteers with preserving their rights to pursue legal sanctions against the perpetrators of the crime. It is very important that Volunteers report incidents as they occur, not only to protect their peer Volunteers, but also to preserve the future right to prosecute. Should Volunteers decide later in the process that they want to proceed with the prosecution of their assailant, this option may no longer exist if the evidence of the event has not been preserved at the time of the incident.

Crime Data for Togo

Crime data and statistics for Togo, which are updated yearly, are available at the following link: http://www.peacecorps.gov/countrydata/togo.

Few Peace Corps Volunteers are victims of serious crimes and crimes that do occur overseas are investigated and prosecuted by local authorities through the local courts system. If you are the victim of a crime, you will decide if you wish to pursue prosecution. If you decide to prosecute, Peace Corps will be there to assist you. One of our tasks is to ensure you are fully informed of your options and understand how the local legal process works. Peace Corps will help you ensure your rights are protected to the fullest extent possible under the laws of the country.

If you are the victim of a serious crime, you will learn how to get to a safe location as quickly as possible and contact your Peace Corps office. It's important that you notify Peace Corps as soon as you can so Peace Corps can provide you with the help you need.

Volunteer Safety Support in Togo

The Peace Corps' approach to safety is a five-pronged plan to help you stay safe during your service and includes the following: information sharing, Volunteer training, site selection criteria, a detailed emergency action plan, and protocols for addressing safety and security incidents. Togo's in-country safety program is outlined below.

The Peace Corps/Togo office will keep you informed of any issues that may impact Volunteer safety through **information sharing**. Regular updates will be provided in Volunteer newsletters and in memorandums from the country director. In the event of a critical situation or emergency, you will be contacted through the emergency communication network. An important component of the capacity of Peace Corps to keep you informed is your buy-in to the partnership concept with the Peace Corps staff. It is expected that you will do your part in ensuring that Peace Corps staff members are kept apprised of your movements in-country so they are able to inform you.

Volunteer training will include sessions on specific safety and security issues in Togo. This training will prepare you to adopt a culturally appropriate lifestyle and exercise judgment that promotes safety and reduces risk in your home, at work, and while traveling. Safety training is offered throughout service and is integrated into the language, cross-cultural aspects, health, and other components of training. You will be expected to successfully complete all training competencies in a variety of areas, including safety and security, as a condition of service.

Certain **site selection criteria** are used to determine safe housing for Volunteers before their arrival. The Peace Corps staff works closely with host communities and counterpart agencies to help prepare them for a Volunteer's arrival and to establish expectations of their respective roles in supporting the Volunteer. Each site is inspected before the Volunteer's arrival to ensure placement in appropriate, safe, and secure housing and worksites. Site selection is based, in part, on any relevant site history; access to medical, banking, postal, and other essential services; availability of communications, transportation, and markets; different housing options and living arrangements; and other Volunteer support needs.

You will also learn about Peace Corps/Togo's **detailed emergency action plan,** which is implemented in the event of civil or political unrest or a natural disaster. When you arrive at your site, you will complete and submit a site locator form with your address, contact information, and a map to your house. If there is a security threat, you will gather with other Volunteers in Togo at predetermined locations until the situation is resolved or the Peace Corps decides to evacuate.

Finally, in order for the Peace Corps to be fully responsive to the needs of Volunteers, it is imperative that Volunteers immediately report any security incident to the Peace Corps office. The Peace Corps has established **protocols for addressing safety and security incidents** in a timely and appropriate manner, and it collects and evaluates safety and security data to track trends and develop strategies to minimize risks to future Volunteers.

DIVERSITY AND CROSS-CULTURAL ISSUES

In fulfilling its mandate to share the face of America with host countries, the Peace Corps is making special efforts to assure that all of America's richness is reflected in the Volunteer corps. More Americans of color are serving in today's Peace Corps than at any time in recent history. Differences in race, ethnic background, age, religion, and sexual orientation are expected and welcomed among our Volunteers. Part of the Peace Corps' mission is to help dispel any notion that Americans are all of one origin or race and to establish that each of us is as thoroughly American as the other despite our many differences.

Our diversity helps us accomplish that goal. In other ways, however, it poses challenges. In Togo, as in other Peace Corps host countries, Volunteers' behavior, lifestyle, background, and beliefs are judged in a cultural context very different from their own. Certain personal perspectives or characteristics commonly accepted in the United States may be quite uncommon, unacceptable, or even repressed in Togo.

Outside of Togo's capital, residents of rural communities have had relatively little direct exposure to other cultures, races, religions, and lifestyles. What people view as typical American behavior or norms may be a misconception, such as the belief that all Americans are rich and have blond hair and blue eyes. The people of Togo are justly known for their generous hospitality to foreigners; however, members of the community in which you will live may display a range of reactions to cultural differences that you present.

To ease the transition and adapt to life in Togo, you may need to make some temporary, yet fundamental compromises in how you present yourself as an American and as an individual. For example, female trainees and Volunteers may not be able to exercise the independence available to them in the United States; political discussions need to be handled with great care; and some of your personal beliefs may best remain undisclosed. You will need to develop techniques and personal strategies for coping with these and other limitations. The Peace Corps staff will lead diversity and sensitivity discussions during pre-service training and will be on call to provide support, but the challenge ultimately will be your own.

Overview of Diversity in Togo

The Peace Corps staff in Togo recognizes the adjustment issues that come with diversity and will endeavor to provide support and guidance. During pre-service training, several sessions will be held to discuss diversity and coping mechanisms. We look forward to having male and female Volunteers from a variety of races, ethnic groups, ages, religions, and sexual orientations, and hope that you will become part of a diverse group of Americans who take pride in supporting one another and demonstrating the richness of American culture.

What Might a Volunteer Face?

Possible Issues for Female Volunteers

Americans working in Togo face cultural adjustments in understanding and addressing prejudices and stereotypes held about them. Unfortunately, the rather lurid films available in Togo, plus society's general attitude toward women, may cause some Togolese to view female Volunteers as "loose" or "available." Togolese men may misinterpret friendly and open gestures by female Volunteers as an invitation to something more serious.

Friendships with Togolese men should have clear boundaries in the beginning. Unlike in the U.S., there is less of a concept that a completely platonic relationship can exist between men and women. To be treated respectfully, female Volunteers may find that they will have to curb some of the activities they were used to in the United States. Late-night socializing with Togolese colleagues is not recommended. Neither is inviting any man you do not know well into your house for any reason if you are alone. Fortunately, you can entertain male guests without giving them—or the community—the wrong idea by remaining in the family compound and ensuring that several family members or neighborhood children are with you and your guest at all times.

It is better to play it safe, especially at the beginning of your service, rather than to be caught in a situation where a Togolese colleague is expecting sex instead of a friendly chat when he comes to visit. It is also a very good idea to make friends with the women in your family and/or neighborhood as soon as possible. Not only will these friendships probably be immensely informative and rewarding, but spending time with women will also prevent unwelcome or inappropriate attention from men.

Possible Issues for Volunteers of Color

Though unconsciously, many Togolese expect that American Volunteers will be white, Volunteers in Togo who are of ethnic minority backgrounds will generally not find overt biases. However, Togolese may make some stereotypic assumptions. For example, most Asian-American Volunteers will automatically be considered Chinese and Kung Fu experts. An African-American Volunteer may first be mistaken for a Ghanaian or Nigerian because of an Anglicized French accent. They may be expected to learn local languages more quickly than other Peace Corps Volunteers and may even be asked about their tribal languages and customs.

Possible Issues for Senior Volunteers

Respect comes with age in traditional Togolese society, so being a senior is generally an advantage. Volunteers in their early 20s find that they may have to make an extra effort to be accepted as professional colleagues since, very often, Togolese of that age are still pursuing their education.

Possible Issues for Married Couple Volunteers

During pre-service training, accommodations are available with the host families for married couples in the same program. If they are assigned to different programs, they will live in different villages, but they can be together on weekends. Once the couple swears-in and goes to their site, they will live together in the same house and community.

Sometimes it is only one of the spouses who really wanted to be a Peace Corps Volunteer and the other just came along in accompaniment. If this is the case, both husband and wife should be very sure they want to serve as Volunteers before committing to do so.

The challenges facing Volunteers (adapting to a different culture, learning a language, working out the details of a job) may be experienced differently by each spouse, but they will both find similar and different rewards as well. A good sense of humor and a lot of communication and patience will be required of couples serving together.

Possible Issues for Gay, Lesbian, or Bisexual Volunteers

Homosexuality is not publicly discussed or acknowledged in Togolese society. Since acceptance in the rural community is part and parcel to a successful Peace Corps experience in Togo, Volunteers with alternative sexual orientations generally choose not to openly discuss their sexual orientation in their villages. Gay and lesbian Volunteers have, however, successfully and safely worked in Togo.

A recommended resource for support and advice prior to and during your service is the Lesbian, Gay, Bisexual & Transgender U.S. Peace Corps Alumni website at www.lgbrpcv.org.

Possible Religious Issues for Volunteers

There are three major religions in Togo: Christianity, Islam, and Animism. People with different religious backgrounds than these three may have difficulty practicing their religion. Being perceived as having no religion at all may not be understood.

Possible Issues for Volunteers With Disabilities

As part of the medical clearance process, the Peace Corps Office of Medical Services determined that you were physically and emotionally capable, with or without reasonable accommodations, to perform a full tour of Volunteer service in Togo without unreasonable risk of harm to yourself or interruption of service. The Peace Corps/Togo staff will work with disabled Volunteers to make reasonable accommodations for them in training, housing, jobsites, or other areas to enable them to serve safely and effectively.

Togolese are very direct and physical disabilities are likely to be pointed out and discussed openly. It should be noted, however, that there is no judgment attached to the comments. It is rather a case of stating the obvious.

For the most part, public facilities in Togo are unequipped to accommodate persons with disabilities. However, the Peace Corps/Togo staff will work with any disabled Volunteers to make reasonable accommodations for them in training, housing, jobsites, or other areas to enable them to serve safely and effectively.

Frequently Asked Questions

This list has been compiled by Volunteers serving in Togo and is based on their experience. Use it as an informal guide in making your own list, bearing in mind that each experience is individual. There is no perfect list! You obviously cannot bring everything on the list, so consider those items that make the most sense to you personally and professionally. You can always have things sent to you later. As you decide what to bring, keep in mind that you have a 100-pound weight limit on baggage. And remember, you can get almost everything you need in Togo.

How much luggage am I allowed to bring to Togo?

Most airlines have baggage size and weight limits and assess charges for transport of baggage that exceeds those limits. The Peace Corps has its own size and weight limits and will not pay the cost of transport for baggage that exceeds these limits. The Peace Corps' allowance is two checked pieces of luggage with combined dimensions of both pieces not to exceed 107 inches (length + width + height) and a carry-on bag with dimensions of no more than 45 inches. Checked baggage should not exceed 100 pounds total with a maximum weight of 50 pounds for any one bag.

Peace Corps Volunteers are not allowed to take pets, weapons, explosives, radio transmitters (shortwave radios are permitted), automobiles, or motorcycles to their overseas assignments. Do not pack flammable materials or liquids such as lighter fluid, cleaning solvents, hair spray, or aerosol containers. This is an important safety precaution.

What is the electric current in Togo?

Togo is on a 220-volt system as is found throughout much of Europe.

How much money should I bring?

Volunteers are expected to live at the same level as the people in their community. You will be given a settling-in allowance and a monthly living allowance, which should cover your expenses. Volunteers often wish to bring additional money for vacation travel to other countries. Credit cards and traveler's checks are preferable to cash. If you choose to bring extra money, bring the amount that will suit your own travel plans and needs.

When can I take vacation and have people visit me?

Each Volunteer accrues two vacation days per month of service (excluding training). Leave may not be taken during training, the first three months of service, or the last three months of service, except in conjunction with an authorized emergency leave. Family and friends are welcome to visit you after pre-service training and the first three months of service as long as their stay does not interfere with your work. Extended stays at your site are not encouraged and may require permission from your country director. The Peace Corps is not able to provide your visitors with visa, medical, or travel assistance.

Will my belongings be covered by insurance?

The Peace Corps does not provide insurance coverage for personal effects; Volunteers are ultimately responsible for the safekeeping of their personal belongings. However, you can purchase personal property insurance before you leave. If you wish, you may contact your own insurance company; additionally, insurance application forms will be provided, and we encourage you to consider them carefully. Volunteers should not ship or take valuable items overseas. Jewelry, watches, radios, cameras, and expensive appliances are subject to loss, theft, and breakage, and in many places, satisfactory maintenance and repair services are not available.

Do I need an international driver's license?

Volunteers in Togo do not need an international driver's license because they are prohibited from operating privately owned motorized vehicles. Most urban travel is by bus or taxi. Rural travel ranges from buses and minibuses to trucks, bicycles, and lots of walking. On very rare occasions, a Volunteer may be asked to drive a sponsor's vehicle, but this can occur only with prior written permission from the country director. Should this occur, the Volunteer may obtain a local driver's license. A U.S. driver's license will facilitate the process, so bring it with you just in case.

What should I bring as gifts for Togo friends and my host family?

This is not a requirement. A token of friendship is sufficient. Some gift suggestions include knickknacks for the house; pictures, books, or calendars of American scenes; souvenirs from your area; hard candies that will not melt or spoil; or photos to give away.

Where will my site assignment be when I finish training and how isolated will I be?

Peace Corps trainees are not assigned to individual sites until after they have completed pre-service training. This gives Peace Corps staff the opportunity to assess each trainee's technical and language skills prior to assigning sites, in addition to finalizing site selections with their ministry counterparts. If feasible, you may have the opportunity to provide input on your site preferences, including geographical location, distance from other Volunteers, and living conditions. However, keep in mind that many factors influence the site selection process and that the Peace Corps cannot guarantee placement where you would ideally like to be. Most Volunteers live in small towns or in rural villages and are usually within one hour from another Volunteer. Some sites require a 10- to 12-hour drive from the capital. There is at least one Volunteer based in each of the regional capitals and about five to eight Volunteers in the capital Lomé.

How can my family contact me in an emergency?

The Peace Corps' Counseling and Outreach Unit (COU) provides assistance in handling emergencies affecting trainees and Volunteers or their families. Before leaving the United States, instruct your family to notify the Counseling and Outreach Unit immediately if an emergency arises, such as a serious illness or death of a family member. During normal business hours, the number for the Counseling and Outreach Unit is 855.855.1961, then select option 2; or directly at 202-692-1470. After normal business hours and on weekends and holidays, the COU duty officer can be reached at the above number. For non-emergency questions, your family can get information from your country desk staff at the Peace Corps by calling 855.855.1961.

Can I call home from Togo?

There are many private telephone booths, called *cabines*, throughout Togo. You can make and receive calls from the phone booths. The price varies depending on the country you are calling and whether you are calling another landline or a cell phone. International calls are quite expensive. You can find alternative solutions in larger towns or the capital city, using such things as Voice Over IP to lower the costs. It is free to receive phone calls on a cellular phone, so many Volunteers ask their families to call them on their personal cell phones (or they borrow one to receive a call).

Should I bring a cellular phone with me?

If you decide to bring a cell phone with you, make sure it's a GSM phone, that you have a power converter if needed, that you can remove the back to replace the SIM card, and that you have unlocked the phone before bringing it to Togo. Please contact your service provider in the U.S. prior to departure to receive the codes and instructions for unlocking the phone for eventual use with another GSM service provider.

Cell phones can be purchased in Togo for a price of roughly CFA 15,000 – 20,000 (approximately $30-$40 in U.S. currency) and up. Outgoing Volunteers often sell their cell phones and you can seek a used phone upon your arrival if you do not wish to bring a phone or purchase a new one.

Will there be email and Internet access? Should I bring my computer?

There is Internet connectivity in most of Togo's larger towns. Cyber cafes have popped up all over the country and are relatively inexpensive. An hour of Internet use varies from $1 to $2 per hour. Connection can be slow and unreliable outside of Lomé. In some areas, you may have to wait until there are two to five people wanting to use the Internet before they will open the phone lines.

Many Volunteers decide to bring a personal laptop with them to Togo. They can be very useful (especially for Masters International candidates); however, you are not required to do so for your work. If you do bring a laptop, bring a relatively inexpensive one, and remember that the Peace Corps has no liability if it is lost, stolen, or damaged. We recommend that you take out personal articles insurance for any valuables that you bring with you. We also cannot guarantee that you will have electricity to charge your computer at your site. However, Volunteers without electricity can usually travel an hour or two to charge their computers every few weeks or so, depending on their locations and their work schedules.

Whether you bring a laptop or not, we recommend that you bring a flash drive (USB) or external hard drive for storing data.

WELCOME LETTERS FROM TOGO VOLUNTEERS

Welcome to Peace Corps Togo!

Congratulations again on having been invited to serve in one of the smallest, and proudest, Peace Corps countries in this rewarding sector! Peace Corps Togo will give you the opportunities to do things you never dreamed possible. One of our country's most important philosophies is to focus on volunteer integration in their communities in order to build meaningful relationships to promote positive behavior change related to community health.

Peace Corps places a large emphasis on volunteer integration and building meaningful relationships with host country nationals to achieve these goals – and PC Togo is no different. You will be provided with resources and training to carry out the most effective Volunteer activities of the past, but as an agent of community development, you will also be responsible for learning about your community and catering your future activities to their needs. Your work will evolve out of the particular needs and realities of your community, your background, skills, interests, and collaboration with your community partners.

In essence, no two days will be the same in Togo. So far during my service, I've organized a series of trainings in conjunction with the Red Cross of Togo aimed at promoting social change through masculine engagement; held an HIV/AIDS themed regional computer camp for high school students to promote healthy life practices; and taught a health/life skills class at the middle school level. I've also had the opportunity to participate in one of Togo's nationwide projects called Camp Espoir, a summer camp for children affected/infected by HIV/AIDS and vaccination campaigns in conjunction with the World Health Organization. The opportunities for work are endless and no two volunteers have the same experience.

There wasn't much I could have done before coming to Togo to prepare myself for the experience of being a Peace Corps Volunteer. Aside from what we all "think" the Peace Corps will be, the reality is that it is entirely up to each individual to determine their experience. The best parts of this job, in my opinion, aren't simply the amazing work opportunities - it's the conversations with friends and counterparts at post, learning to express yourself in another language, sharing American culture with Togolese and sharing a bit of Togo with your friends and loved ones stateside. They are so many aspects of this that are enriching in so many ways, most of them subtle and easily overlooked if one is not careful. All you really have to do in order to be "ready" for the Peace Corps is give yourself the permission to experience it fully: the good, the bad, and the incredible.

I am confident that you will find this experience worthwhile and fulfilling. Get ready for the challenge, but you will be in the very best company. Best of luck to you all and as we say in Togo "du courage!"

Ryan Aghabozorg
Community Health and AIDS Prevention Volunteer

Dear Incoming Volunteers,

Welcome to the Peace Corps! There is not much that someone can say to prepare you for such an experience, but that's the whole point—to experience it for yourself!

I'll start with the basics. I live in the Maritime region, in a village of about 30,000 people, called Agbelouve. I have electricity, a well in my compound, and an incredible host family. I teach two classes at a combined middle school/high school, with 105 students in one class and 85 in the other. Teaching is fun; it is tiring; it is rewarding and it is certainly difficult, but the school provides a degree of community that is not easy to find in your first few months, even your first year, at post.

Working at a school provides easy and accessible work opportunities. Seven months into post, I have coached girls' and boys' soccer teams, I host a Men as Partners Club, a Girls in Science Club, a Peer Educator Club, and have recently started an English Club and Girls in Commerce Club. My school has over 1,000 students, so finding motivated and interested students to participate is not terribly difficult. Thanks to the great work of the volunteer before me, I have 6 wonderful and motivated work-counterparts, all of which help me with a variety of things, from speaking local language to gender promotion activities to eating proper Togolese food. During the summer vacation I plan on working on some projects in village, as well as national projects such as an English camp, and continuing to tutor English to friends and counterparts in village.

Daniel Brown
English and Gender Education Volunteer

Dear Future Togo Volunteers,

Greetings from Togo! This tiny country has been my home for a year and a half, but I still find myself continually adjusting to new experiences. I completed my volunteer application while spending my last year of college in Italy. After returning to the States for a few weeks, I boarded a plane to yet another foreign destination, this one in West Africa, to see just how much culture shock I could take. Throughout Pre-Service Training (PST) and during my first few months in village I found myself undergoing numerous physical and behavioral changes: rushing to the latrine less as I adapted to the local pâte (corn paste) with fish sauce, saying 'doucement' (go slowly) to caution friends going into hazardous situations, and looking forward to bucket showers after working in the field all morning. The changes in diet, language, and work habits were made tougher to handle than those I confronted in Italy because I became the center of attention whenever I stepped outside the door.

Integration into my community has proceeded in two directions. On one side, I've changed. I struggled to learn French and am now grappling with the local language. I've changed my sense of time to set realistic expectations for projects and gotten accustomed to having my host sisters shouting outside my door every night. On the other hand, my community has adapted to me. The Togolese in my village have stopped greeting me with stares and calls of 'Yovo' (white person). Now I can hardly keep my hands on the bars when biking into town because I'm waving to so many smiling neighbors calling out 'Kossi,' my local name. People I work with have gotten used to my strange habit of following up when planning meetings and then arriving on time to start them. These communal changes, on top of the million smaller habits I've developed like sweeping my house and filtering water, have made me more okay being where I am. I'm extending for a third year in Togo. The culture and language continue to fascinate me, the people I work with are dedicated and inspiring, and my primary projects move forward a bit every day. The adjustment never really ends, but I've learned to love the process and I hope that you do too!

Benjamin Bogardus
Environmental Action and Food Security Volunteer

☞ ☜

My favorite time in village is when the sun is setting, when everyone leaves their porches and shady spots to walk around, socialize, and buy supplies for dinner. Danyi-N'digbe, my village of about 2,000 people, feels busiest at 5 P.M. when the weather is breezy and pleasant. I can enjoy a cup of bouille—corn flour porridge—sitting on a bench at the main intersection and watching the grandpas' fiercely competitive peg game. My counterpart usually stops by to say hello, since his wife runs the bouille stand, and we can catch up on the progress of our latrine project, what the subject of our next training will be, or just on the village news.

This summer, I completed a latrine project for families in my village so that more people in N'digbe can have a safe and hygienic place to go to the bathroom. Previously, people used the nearby fields or woods when they needed to do their business. But this is a major cause of diarrheal disease and unsanitary living conditions. My counterpart, a community health volunteer, and I selected eleven sites for composting latrines. In exchange for cement, tin, and other building supplies, families in N'digbe dug pits for the latrines, donated land for latrine sites, and fed the laborers. A critical part of the project was making sure people understood why latrines are important, and how hand washing after going to the bathroom also prevents disease. I am very happy that my community is dedicated to improving hygiene and contributed to the project at every step.

In addition to long term projects, I also have regular activities that keep me busy during the week, such as my work at the local health clinic. The clinic's three-person staff assists the entire village population as well as the surrounding farms, so they really can use the extra help. I enjoy assisting the health workers, who are also my close friends, and I appreciate that my time at the clinic helps improve life in N'digbe. We offer consultations to pregnant mothers, family planning appointments, and now HIV testing, as part of the fight against mother-to-child transmission of HIV/AIDS. Additionally, mothers bring their infants or toddlers once a month to the clinic for vaccinations, baby-weighing, and an informative health discussion given by the nurse and me on healthy nutrition practices for babies, treating diarrhea, and how to prevent malaria.

After spending time at the clinic or doing home visits with my counterpart, I am happy to end the day in my house with my kitten. My best friend in village, one of the students at the nearby middle school, stops by for a few rounds of UNO or to share a meal of fufu and mushroom sauce. And once I blow out my kerosene lantern for the night, I get a perfect view of the stars.

Kate Litvin
Community Health and AIDS Prevention Volunteer

                                ❧ ☙

Dear Future Togo PCVs,

Being a PCV in Togo, West Africa, is a challenging yet rewarding job. Togo is a small yet diverse country, thus the experience of a PCV's service differs depending on their program sector, their village size, and village demographic. As an EAFS volunteer living in northern Togo, I live with no electricity and draw my water from a well near my house. I have my own house, but live in a compound with several houses with welcoming and kind neighbors, along with numerous children running around and asking to draw and practice their lessons on my chalkboard. The weekly market is something of a celebration, where I can meet my friends, greet people and see the colorful vegetables and taste the foods that are produced in my village. I work with various community groups on a variety of different projects. Finding a project that will work well in your community is not always easy, and should not be something that is started quickly without thinking things through and discussing with community members.

Recently, a motivated counterpart and I began a small rabbit raising project to improve the food security of his family. Rabbit production will provide meat for the family, provide money through the selling of rabbits, and also provide the family with rabbit droppings to be used as a natural fertilizer in their gardens. The success of this project is motivating, because though it is small, it has the power to make a large impact on this family, and hopefully the knowledge of rabbit production will be transferred to other families. Participating in activities like the Coverdell World Wide Schools Program also allows me to share information about America with Togolese students, and share information about Togo with American students. Creating a pen pal program allowed us to correspond with American primary school students, sharing drawings, songs, dances, and the students' favorite things. Students in both countries learned that though they are many miles apart and speak different languages, many things in their lives are in fact similar.

Katie Koralesky
Environmental Action and Food Security Volunteer

PACKING LIST

This list has been compiled by Volunteers serving in Togo and is based on their experience. Use it as an informal guide in making your own list, bearing in mind that each experience is individual. There is no perfect list! You obviously cannot bring everything on the list, so consider those items that make the most sense to you personally and professionally. You can always have things sent to you later. As you decide what to bring, keep in mind that you have an 100-pound weight limit on baggage. And remember, you can get almost everything you need in Togo.

General Clothing

Women

- A large supply of underwear and bras. They wear out quickly and take a beating when they are washed. Cotton is best (Bring at least one dozen pairs of underwear. Also, underwire bras are more difficult to wash.)

- Cotton dresses and/or skirts, knee length or longer. Loose cotton dresses can be cooler than a skirt and blouse. (Try to keep in mind that you may want to ride a bike wearing it!)

- Hair bands and barrettes

- Loose fitting cotton tops and T-shirts (nothing too revealing or cropped). Try to stay away from white. It gets dirty fast!

- Tank tops for hot days. (Remember that cultural norms are much more conservative than those in the U.S. You should only wear tank tops while hanging out in your house)

- One pair of jeans (they are hot, but useful). Khakis and/or cotton pants, capris (ankle length or a little shorter) are better

- Cotton socks for jogging or sports (and keeping away mosquitoes). No nylons.

- Shorts (for around the house and sports) – should be knee length if possible (Two or three pairs)

- Cotton bandannas, two or three (Traveling can be dusty)

- A few nice outfits for those two or three special occasions in your village or when visiting regional capitals (nothing heavy, hot, or too revealing). You can have appropriate outfits made here too.

Men

- Jeans (one or two pairs). They can also be purchased cheaply in Togo at used clothing spots.

- Cotton/khaki pants (two pair). You can have pants made here.

- "Zip-off" pants/shorts (easy to wash)

- Cotton shirts. You can have shirts made here.

- Cotton underwear, up to two dozen pairs. (Boxers or boxer briefs are recommended because they allow more air circulation, and fungus can be a problem.)
- One tie, nice shirt, and pants. Cotton socks for jogging or sports and for keeping mosquitoes away. (If you're athletic, bring more.)
- Bermuda shorts (two or three pairs) – for in your house or at the beach
- Baseball cap or bandannas

Men and Women

- Windbreaker or rain slicker//poncho. Umbrellas can be   purchased here.
- Lightweight hooded sweatshirt or long-sleeved shirt for occasional cool evening
- Day pack for shopping; larger backpack for traveling
- Bathing suit
- Catalogs or pictures of clothing you may want copied

Shoes

Men and Women

- One pair of good sandals like Tevas, Reefs, or Chacos. These are good for mud, water, biking, and walking.
- Sneakers/running shoes (especially if you exercise)
- One pair of nice shoes or sandals

Personal Hygiene and Toiletry Items

- U.S. toiletry items (including shampoo, hair conditioner, facial creams, and toners) are available here, but they are expensive. It is a good idea to bring at least a three-month supply to get you through training. Women may want to bring some makeup for special occasions.
- Deodorant, especially if you prefer roll-on or stick.

Miscellaneous

- Luggage that is tough and flexible, such as backpacks plus luggage locks. Have something that will carry your belongings for a weeklong trip.
- Money belt or pouch that can be concealed under clothing or worn on the waist to carry money and other valuables.
- A reliable watch plus batteries. (Water resistant sports watches with washable bands are best.)
- A reliable alarm clock (battery-operated), or a watch with an alarm or a cellphone with these features (usable worldwide and unlocked).

- Swiss Army knife or equivalent (i.e., Leatherman tool)

- Small sewing kit and safety pins

- A favorite hat with wide brim for protection from the sun

- Sunglasses with UV protection

- Camera (small models are more convenient since they are inconspicuous and travel well). Bring a good case for protection from sun and dust.

- Digital cameras are also quite handy. Digital photos can be stored on computers available to Volunteers. (Get the largest memory cards you can.)

- Digital thumb drive. Very useful for transporting digital files between computers. (Remember to bring the "drivers," or any necessary software.)

- Flashlight (or two) with extra bulbs (You can also buy flashlights in Togo).

- Rechargeable batteries and charger. If you plan on bringing rechargeable batteries be sure that your charger will run on 220 volt current, or is multi-voltage. (Solar chargers get mixed reviews from Volunteers.)

- U.S. stamps. You can often have letters mailed in the United States by people traveling there from Lomé.

- A small pillow

- Plastic water bottle for traveling. Nalgene preferred

- Pillowcases and one flat bed sheet. Bring at least one set from home as you will need them right away.

- Hammock (optional)

- Compact, quick drying pack towels. You can buy regular towels in the market.

- Good scissors and nail clippers

- Colored markers, crayons, and construction paper, for making visual aids and playing with kids. These items are available in Togo, but expensive.

- Journal. (paperback style journals are available in Togo)

- Writing paper (small supply, just to get started. There are plenty available in Togo)

- Pens (Bring plenty; the ones here do not last long)

- Duct tape/packing tape (highly recommended)

- Pictures of home. Your Togolese friends will be very interested in seeing what your "former life" was like.

- Maps of the United States and the world

- Mini office supplies (stapler, hole punch, white out, post it notes, sticky tack

- Reading light (a headlamp can also be used as a reading light)

- Calendar/day planner

- Seeds for personal garden (flowers or vegetables – remember the climate is tropical!) (Optional)

- GPRS (voice and data) enabled phone to be able to check email wherever there is cell phone reception. Nokia is most easily configured.

- Shortwave radio or satellite receiver. Stations such as BBC, Voice of America, and Radio France International can be received with a moderate quality shortwave radio.

- Walkman/cassette tape player/hand-held recorder/iPod or MP3 player and favorite tapes/CDs, plus extra blank tapes and portable speakers

- Hobby items such as sketch book, sewing/crochet needles, paints, sticky tax for hanging pictures and maps

- Surge protector/voltage converter for any expensive electronics such as laptop computer, iPod, or MP3 player.

- Games, such as Scrabble, chess, UNO and Frisbee. Ordinary playing cards abound.

- Frisbee, soccer ball, hackey sac, etc.

- Musical instruments – harmonica, guitar (bring extra guitar strings)

- One or two books. There are many books in English in the Peace Corps office library and the libraries at the regional transit houses. We are, however, short on current bestsellers and books (in English) by African authors.

- Ziploc bags. At least one box of various sizes.

- High quality dish towels (1 or 2, they are available here)

All of the items below can be purchased in Lomé at relatively competitive (to the U.S.) prices.

- Plastic food storage containers, a good can opener, frying pans, and other kitchen tools for baking (spatula, bake pans, measuring cups).

- Your favorite spices or sauce packets. Local markets may have bay leaves, chili peppers, garlic, anise, and peppercorns. Other spices such as curry, oregano, etc., can be bought in Lomé. Seasoning packets for pasta are highly recommended, as are cinnamon and burrito/taco spices.

- Garlic press

- Powdered drinks such as Kool-Aid or Crystal Lite. (The medical unit provides Gatorade.) You can find sweetened powdered drink mixes in Togo.

- Contact lens solution; two-year supply

- If you take prescription medicine, bring a three-month supply.

- Eyeglasses (two pairs).

- Sting Eze/Bite Relief. You will want a lot of this.

PRE-DEPARTURE CHECKLIST

The following list consists of suggestions for you to consider as you prepare to live outside the United States for two years. Not all items will be relevant to everyone, and the list does not include everything you should make arrangements for.

Family

- Notify family that they can call the Peace Corps' Office of Special Services at any time if there is a critical illness or death of a family member (24-hour telephone number: 1-855-855-1961, then press 2; or directly at 202-692-1470).

- Give the Peace Corps' *On the Home Front* handbook to family and friends.

Passport/Travel

- Forward to the Peace Corps travel office all paperwork for the Peace Corps passport and visas.

- Verify that your luggage meets the size and weight limits for international travel.

- Obtain a personal passport if you plan to travel after your service ends. (Your Peace Corps passport will expire three months after you finish your service, so if you plan to travel longer, you will need a regular passport.)

Medical/Health

- Complete any needed dental and medical work.

- If you wear glasses, bring two pairs.

- Arrange to bring a three-month supply of all medications (including birth control pills) you are currently taking.

Insurance

- Make arrangements to maintain life insurance coverage.

- Arrange to maintain supplemental health coverage while you are away. (Even though the Peace Corps is responsible for your health care during Peace Corps service overseas, it is advisable for people who have pre-existing conditions to arrange for the continuation of their supplemental health coverage. If there is a lapse in coverage, it is often difficult and expensive to be reinstated.)

- Arrange to continue Medicare coverage if applicable.

Personal Papers

- Bring a copy of your certificate of marriage or divorce.

Voting

- Register to vote in the state of your home of record. (Many state universities consider voting and payment of state taxes as evidence of residence in that state.)

- Obtain a voter registration card and take it with you overseas.

- Arrange to have an absentee ballot forwarded to you overseas.

Personal Effects

- Purchase personal property insurance to extend from the time you leave your home for service overseas until the time you complete your service and return to the United States.

Financial Management

- Keep a bank account in your name in the U.S.

- Obtain student loan deferment forms from the lender or loan service.

- Execute a Power of Attorney for the management of your property and business.

- Arrange for deductions from your readjustment allowance to pay alimony, child support, and other debts through the Office of Volunteer Financial Operations at 855.855.1961, extension 1770.

- Place all important papers – mortgages, deeds, stocks, and bonds – in a safe deposit box or with an attorney or other caretaker.

www.ingramcontent.com/pod-product-compliance
Lightning Source LLC
Chambersburg PA
CBHW081754280526
45789CB00008B/2849